PIRANHA

by Ann Ingalls

Content Consultant
William L. Fink
Curator of Fishes, Museum of Zoology
Professor, Department of Ecology and Evolutionary Biology
University of Michigan

CORE
LIBRARY

Published by ABDO Publishing Company, PO Box 398166, Minneapolis, MN 55439. Copyright © 2014 by Abdo Consulting Group, Inc. International copyrights reserved in all countries. No part of this book may be reproduced in any form without written permission from the publisher. The Core Library™ is a trademark and logo of ABDO Publishing Company.

Printed in the United States of America,
North Mankato, Minnesota
052013
092013

♻ THIS BOOK CONTAINS AT LEAST 10% RECYCLED MATERIALS.

Editor: Lauren Coss
Series Designer: Becky Daum

Library of Congress Control Number: 2013932507

Cataloging-in-Publication Data
Ingalls, Ann.
 Piranha / Ann Ingalls.
  p. cm. -- (Great Predators)
ISBN 978-1-61783-951-1 (lib. bdg.)
ISBN 978-1-62403-016-1 (pbk.)
Includes bibliographical references and index.
1. Piranhas--Juvenile literature. 2. Predatory animals--Juvenile literature.
I. Title.
597--dc23

                                            2013932507

Photo Credits: Uli Deck/picture-alliance/dpa/AP Images, cover, 1; Gamma-Rapho/Getty Images, 4; Mikhail Kokhanchikov/iStockphoto, 7, 43; Shutterstock Images, 9, 45; age fotostock/SuperStock, 10, 36; Maxim Tupikov/Shutterstock Images, 12; Paul Zahl/National Geographic/Getty Images, 15, 22, 26; iStockphoto, 17; Belinda Images/SuperStock, 18; Red Line Editorial, 20, 31; NHPA/SuperStock, 24; Minden Pictures/SuperStock, 28; Biosphoto/SuperStock, 30; Thinkstock, 32; NaturePL/SuperStock, 39; Tomasz Pietryszek/iStockphoto, 40

CONTENTS

CHAPTER ONE

HUNGRY FISH

S un shimmers through the heavy canopy over the lagoon. It is dry season in the Amazon. Water levels of the river homes of the piranhas are low. A school of red-bellied piranhas have been trapped in a still pool of water for weeks. Before long, all the food in the pool is gone. Now piranhas will eat anything that enters the water.

Piranhas strip a lamb carcass at a French aquarium.

Piranhas' Name

Piranhas are named after their razor-sharp teeth. Their name comes from the Tupi-Guarani Indian people, who are native to Brazil. In their language, the word *piro* means "fish" and *ranha* means "tooth" or "scissors." The right way to say the word piranha is *puh-RON-uh.*

A heron chick perches on a branch over the water. It is just learning to fly, and it is not very skillful. It begins to totter and slips into the water. Splash! All at once, a feeding frenzy begins.

The water churns red with blood as the piranhas wildly attack the heron. The hungry fish strip the little bird of its flesh in minutes. Sometimes they accidentally take bites out of each other while feeding. The feast is over in a matter of minutes. Nothing but bones and a few feathers remain.

A Fierce Fish

Piranhas are freshwater fish that are famous for their razor-sharp teeth. Most are approximately eight inches (20 cm) long. But they can grow to be up to

Chromatophore cells give some piranhas distinctive red eyes.

18 inches (46 cm) long. They vary in color from silvery to olive-green to blue-black. Some have orange or red bellies. Piranha scales look like tiles on a roof. Above the scales is a layer of skin that gives off mucus, which makes the fish feel slimy. The mucus prevents infection. When a piranha gets cut or scratched, scales grow back quickly.

Tiny cells called chromatophores give the scales colors. These chromatophore cells can give some species ruby-red eyes. Older fish often become darker and less intense in color. Some species of piranha have a spot called a humeral blotch near their gills.

All piranhas have fins that help them swim. When piranhas swim, they fold their fins close to their bodies. Sometimes they flick their fins to change their position in the water.

Most piranhas have rounded heads and small jaws full of sharp, triangular teeth. They have strong jaws that are short and wide. They use these jaws to tear the flesh off their prey. But even piranhas cannot eat a large animal by themselves. They often collect in large schools during the dry season.

Red-bellied Piranhas

The most famous kind of piranha is the red-bellied piranha. This species can grow up to 12 inches (30 cm) in length. Red-bellied piranhas will eat just about anything. They feast on other fish and sometimes large animals, such as cattle. But this does not happen very often. Red-bellied piranhas prefer prey that is only a bit larger or smaller than they are.

Red-bellied piranhas are one of the most common species of piranha.

Then they nip off scales or bits of flesh from their prey until the group devours the animal.

There are at least 30 species of piranha. And scientists believe there are likely many more species. Piranhas are native to lowland South American rivers and lakes. These fierce fish can have a scary reputation because of their ability to eat animals many times their size. But only four or five species

Red-bellied piranhas also eat the carcasses of animals that are already dead, such as this bird.

of piranha eat large animals live. Most prefer small animals, such as insects, fish, birds, and snakes.

Piranhas are useful in the Amazonian waters. They prey on weak and sick animals so only the strong survive. Many piranhas are scavengers. They eat animals that are already dead. Some piranhas feed on plant material. Most are quite harmless to humans.

US President Theodore Roosevelt went on a hunting expedition in Brazil in 1913. From the bank of the Amazon River, he watched piranhas attack a cow. Later he described the fish:

> *They are the most ferocious fish in the world. Even the most formidable fish, the sharks or the barracudas, usually attack things smaller than themselves. But the piranhas habitually attack things much larger than themselves. They will snap a finger off a hand incautiously trailed in the water; they mutilate swimmers—in every river town in Paraguay there are men who have been thus mutilated; they will rend and devour alive any wounded man or beast; for blood in the water excites them to madness. They will tear wounded wild fowl to pieces; and bite off the tails of big fish as they grow exhausted when fighting after being hooked.*

Source: Theodore Roosevelt. Through the Brazilian Wilderness. *New York: Charles Scribner's Sons, 1914. Print. 41.*

What's the Big Idea?

Read this passage carefully. What is Roosevelt's main point about piranhas? Pick out two details he uses to make his point. How do these details support Roosevelt's main idea? How does Roosevelt's description compare to the information you learned in this chapter?

CHAPTER TWO

A PIRANHA'S LIFE

In December heavy rains begin falling in the Amazon River Basin. Water levels begin to rise. Piranhas usually breed near the end of the rainy season, typically in April or May. Scientists aren't sure of the age at which piranhas are ready to breed. Male piranhas often choose a breeding site among the water plants. The male begins to follow a female. Then courtship begins.

Piranhas usually breed in the spring.

The male makes a nest in the river bottom by scooping out a depression. Plants are also often added to the nest. Once the nest is built, the female lays her eggs. This is called spawning. It may take several hours for a piranha to spawn. The female lays several hundred to several thousand eggs, depending on the species. The male fertilizes the eggs.

Most scientists believe both parents guard the eggs. Hatching time can vary from two to five days. The time depends on the water temperature and the species of piranha.

From Fry to Full-Grown Fish

Baby piranhas are known as fry. The little fry's first

How to Speak Piranha

Piranhas can produce a drumming, croaking, or buzzing sound. This may be their way of sharing information. They do this using swim bladders. Swim bladders are gas-filled organs inside the piranhas. This bladder also works a little like a flotation device. The piranha can control the amount of gas in the bladder. This allows piranhas to rise or fall in the water.

Baby piranhas are fed ground meat at an Ohio zoo.

meal is the yolk sac of their eggs. The fry begin to swim a few days after hatching. Then they leave the nest to look for food and shelter among floating plants or flooded meadows.

When tiny piranhas hatch from their eggs, they have sharp teeth. At first the fry eat small insects and crustaceans. But by the time the fry are nearly two inches (5 cm) in length, they are big enough to feed on fins and flesh of other fish that come close.

As they get bigger, some species of piranha swim in groups called shoals. Most shoals have approximately 20 fish. But sometimes piranhas hunt in shoals that are much larger. Young piranhas hang around the outside of the shoal, where they can feed easily. As they mature, the fish move into the center of the shoal, where it is safer from predators.

Scientists aren't sure how long piranhas can survive in the wild. They think most piranhas live to be at least five years old. But in captivity piranhas may live to be as old as 15.

Pet Piranhas

Believe it or not, these fierce fish are very popular as pets. Red-bellied piranhas are one of the most popular species of piranha to keep as a pet. Piranhas can be tough pets to keep. They need large tanks with warm water. They can grow very large for a pet fish. When people try to mate piranhas in captivity, the fish often attack or even kill one another.

Piranhas are popular pets because of their bright colors.

CHAPTER THREE

KINGS OF THE AMAZON

Piranhas have special characteristics that help make them top predators in the Amazon's waters. These characteristics help them hunt down their prey.

Fishy Senses

Piranhas have an excellent sense of smell. They can even smell blood in the water. Piranhas also have good eyesight. Piranhas' eyes are on the sides of

With powerful jaws and sharp teeth, piranhas are some of the top predators of their underwater homes.

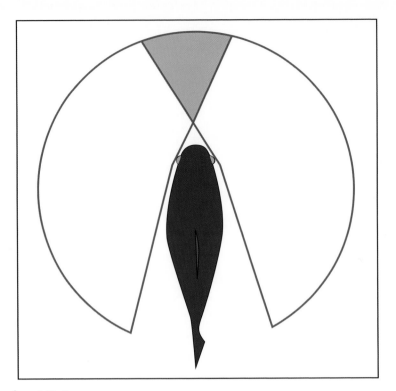

Piranha Vision

Take a look at the diagram of the piranha and its line of vision. The blue section indicates the area the piranha cannot see. How would this line of vision help the piranha hunt? What might be some limitations to a piranha's eyesight?

their heads. This means the fish cannot see directly in front of themselves. However, they have a large field of vision on their sides. They can even see some movement that goes on behind them. This helps them become aware of danger and possible prey in all directions.

Piranhas also have excellent hearing. In fact, it is nearly as good as human hearing. This is much better than most fish. Piranhas listen for the sounds of splashing in the water. This might mean a hurt or struggling animal is nearby. They can also hear the barking, croaking, and other sounds made by fellow piranhas. Scientists aren't sure why piranhas make these noises. But they think the fish might use these sounds when fighting with or confronting other piranhas.

Small hair cells grow in the scales along the piranhas' sides. The hair and pores together are called the lateral line. The hairs sense motion in the water

Bite Power

Bite force measures the amount of pressure an animal puts on something when that animal snaps its jaws shut on it. Piranhas' jaws are super strong. In fact, a piranha has a bite force of 70 pounds (32 kg). That is a lot of power for such a small fish. A piranha's bite force is more than 30 times its body weight. This is stronger than a great white shark's bite force relative to its body weight.

A group of hungry piranhas are capable of stripping animals as large as cattle to the bone.

around the fish, alerting them to enemies, prey, or falling seeds and fruit.

Terrifying Teeth

A piranha's lower jaw is packed with huge teeth. Most of the time, their thick lips hide the teeth. These pointed teeth are razor sharp and interlock. They are not made to crush, tear, or hold on to prey. Instead, they clip off pieces of flesh or fins.

Piranhas shed their teeth throughout their lifetime. If a piranha loses a single tooth, the rest of the fish's teeth will soon fall out and be replaced by a new set of teeth. The replacement set is already formed in the piranha's gums. Piranhas' teeth usually fall out in sections. That way the piranha is

Piranha Scissors

People who are native to the Amazon rely on piranhas for many different reasons. They eat the fish. They also use piranha teeth to make tools and weapons. Amazonian natives use dried piranha jaws to make a tool that looks somewhat like scissors and a knife. In some parts of South America, scissors are known as "piranhas."

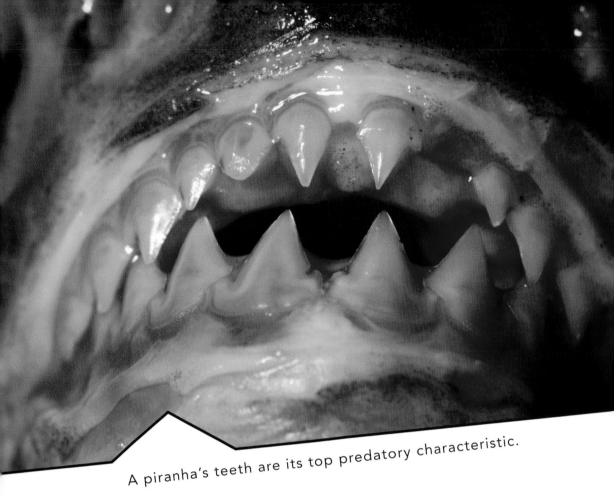

A piranha's teeth are its top predatory characteristic.

never completely toothless. The new teeth grow in just a few days.

Despite these predatory features, piranhas don't always eat live prey. Many piranhas are scavengers. Some species of piranha feed by nipping off bits of fins and scales of other fish. This is called lepidophagy. The prey fish will swim away and usually heal completely.

Most piranhas never kill large animals. Attacks on people are rare, although some people who swim in the Amazon's waters have lost fingers and toes to these hungry fish.

Feeding Frenzy

Sometimes food becomes scarce. When this happens, piranhas might join together to attack a large animal. Red-bellied piranhas sometimes hunt in groups of more than 100. Sometimes a member of the group will attack prey on its own. The other piranhas in the group are attracted by the smells and action of the attack. They often join in.

This type of group attack is known as a feeding frenzy. Several groups of piranhas may join in a

Megapiranha

More than 10 million years ago, the piranha's giant extinct relative may have had a stronger bite for its body weight than a *tyrannosaurus rex*. *Megapiranha paranensis*, or megapiranha, was one of the top predators of its day. It was also bigger than modern piranhas. Scientists believe it might have been more than two feet (0.6 m) long. The big fish may have weighed 22 pounds (10 kg).

The water churns as hungry South American piranhas eat a capybara, a large South American rodent.

feeding frenzy if a large animal is attacked. Piranhas don't chew. They simply take bites and swallow. Every fish in the feeding frenzy rushes in to take a bite. Then each fish swims out of the way so others can feed. The hungry piranhas take turns, constantly changing position, until the unlucky animal has been stripped to the bone.

In 2012 a group of scientists published an article about a study they did on wild piranhas. They measured the bite forces of different fish compared to their sizes. They hoped studying modern piranhas would help them learn more about the extinct megapiranha:

> [A] bite force of 320 N in Serrasalmus rhombeus [black piranha] is the strongest yet recorded for any bony or cartilaginous fish to date, and is nearly three times greater than the bite force of an equivalent size American alligator. [The] data demonstrate that S. rhombeus can bite with a force more than 30 times its weight, a remarkable feat yet unmatched among vertebrates. However, it should be noted that there was some variation in our . . . bite force data among similar sized individuals that was likely caused by some individuals under-performing due to stress or fatigue.

Source: Justin R. Grubich et al. "Mega-Bites: Extreme Jaw Forces of Living and Extinct Piranhas (Serrasalmidae)." Scientific Reports. Nature Publishing Group, December 20, 2012. Web. Accessed March 4, 2013.

Consider Your Audience

This passage was written for a scientific audience. How would you adapt it for a different audience, such as your parents, your siblings, or your friends? Are there any words you aren't familiar with? Look up these words. Then write a blog post presenting the information from the passage to a new audience.

CHAPTER FOUR

AT HOME WITH PIRANHAS

Piranhas are cold-blooded fish. This means that they get their body heat from the water around them. They cannot survive in cold water. Their habitat is the warm waters of South America's Amazon River and its tributaries. Most live in rivers with a water temperature between 75 and 86 degrees Fahrenheit (24–30°C).

Piranhas spend their lives in the warm, freshwater rivers and streams of South America.

Some piranhas spend their time in calm waters with plenty of plant growth.

Many piranhas make their homes in fast-moving rivers and streams. Others are found in ponds or lakes where the current is not so strong. Piranhas will usually group and breed in these slow-moving

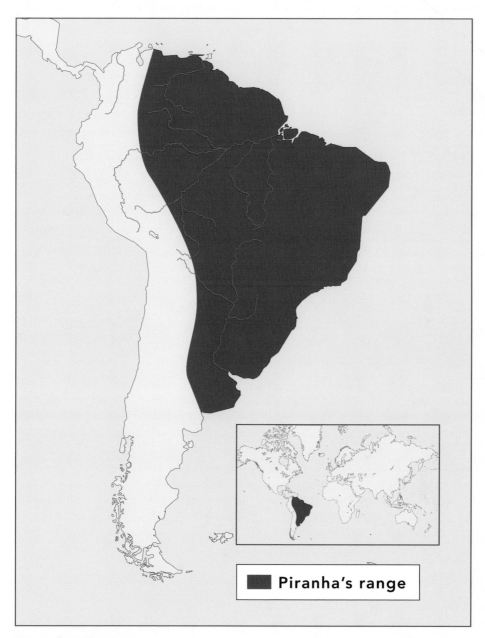

Piranha's range

Piranha Range

Piranhas are native to freshwater rivers in South America.
This map shows the different areas in which piranhas live.
How does the map compare to the information in this
chapter? Why might a piranha live in these areas?

The Amazon River and its rainforest are home to many amazing plants and animals.

waters. Some species of piranhas make their homes in underwater roots of trees and plants.

The Amazon

Piranhas range from northern Argentina to Colombia. They live in the Amazon River and its tributaries. Nowhere else on Earth is quite like the Amazon. It has the largest rainforest and a greater variety of animals than anywhere else in the world.

The rainy season in the Amazon begins in December and lasts until June. During the rainy season, rivers rise and swamp much of the

Amazing Amazon

The Amazon is the second longest river in the world. It flows more than 4,087 miles (6,577 km). The Amazon lies on the equator. Parts of the Amazon get more than 200 inches (500 cm) of rain each year. That rain falls onto the land that is called the Amazon River drainage basin. When rain falls and lands anywhere in the basin, it runs toward lower ground. The lowest place is the Amazon River and its smaller feeding rivers. The Amazon has more water than any other river on Earth.

forest. Most trees bear fruit at this time. A lot of the trees depend upon fish, including piranhas, to spread their seeds by eating them.

A Long Way from Home

Piranhas are native only to South America. But they have been found all over the world. This is because people release unwanted pet piranhas into rivers and lakes far from the Amazon. This can be dangerous to local animals and to the released piranhas. In 2009 a piranha was found in the cold waters of the Devon River in the United Kingdom. The piranha was not able to survive the chilly temperatures. Environment agency workers believed the fish was a former pet because they found sweet corn in its stomach.

The dry season typically lasts from July to November. During this time, the waters of the Amazon run low. Piranhas can become stranded in small pools of water. This is a dangerous time for the piranhas. The trapped fish are vulnerable to predators.

Hungry birds and caimans can easily grab piranhas out of the shallow water. The small pools also run out of food quickly. This is when a feeding frenzy is most likely to happen. The starving fish will eat anything they can get their teeth into. With so little food to choose from, piranhas are more likely to go after larger prey they wouldn't normally attack.

PIRANHAS AS PREY

As fierce as piranhas can be, they are not safe from predators. Young piranhas are part of many other animals' diets. Adult piranhas will even eat younger piranhas.

During the dry season, adult piranhas become trapped in lagoons. Caimans and herons feed on these stranded fish. Other birds, otters, crocodiles,

Humans fish for piranhas both for food and as a sport.

and dolphins will also eat piranhas if they have the chance.

Humans are piranhas' main predators. Many people like to eat piranhas. The fish are caught in nets, in traps, and by hooks and lines. These piranhas are often sold to food markets. Other people like to fish for piranhas for sport, or for fun.

Piranhas are also taken from the wild and sent around the world for the exotic pet trade. Some are killed, dried, and mounted. People use these piranhas as decorations.

Pesky Piranhas

Piranhas are important to their own ecosystem. But they can be a big problem when they are introduced elsewhere. They are dangerous to native fish populations when released into waters outside South America. Piranhas can throw off the balance of their new ecosystem. Because of this, piranhas are now illegal to own in many places. If piranhas are discovered in non-native waters, officials will often poison the piranhas.

Protecting Piranhas

Piranhas are not considered endangered.

A hungry caiman is happy to make a piranha its next meal.

But it is still important for people to work to protect these fish. Piranhas are an important part of their ecosystem. They clean up their environment by eating sick, dying, or dead animals. They control fish populations. Piranhas help to keep the rivers in the Amazon healthy.

Piranhas are fierce predators that play an important role in keeping their river ecosystems healthy.

There is much about piranhas that scientists do not know. It is not even known how many species of piranha there are. These amazing predators may play a more important role in the natural world than we know.

EXPLORE ONLINE

Chapter Five discusses threats to piranhas and why many people fear them. The article at the Web site below discusses some of these topics. As you know, every source is different. How does the information in the Web site compare to the information in this chapter? How do the two sources present information differently? What can you learn from the Web site?

Ferocious Piranhas
www.mycorelibrary.com/piranha

Common Name: Piranha

Scientific Name: *Pygocentrus nattereri*

Average Size: Eight inches (20 cm)

Average Weight: Three pounds (1.3 kg)

Color: Often silvery or olive-green or blue-black; many have orange or red bellies

Diet: Other fish, reptiles, mammals, birds, insects, dead animals, plants, and seeds

Habitat: The Amazon River and its tributaries

Predators: Caimans, crocodiles, birds, other fish, dolphins, and humans

Did You Know?

- Attacks by piranhas on humans are extremely rare.
- If a piranha loses a single tooth, all of its teeth will soon be replaced by a new set.
- A piranha's bite force is greater than that of a great white shark relative to its body weight.

Why Do I Care?

Piranhas are very important predators. They help keep their ecosystems healthy. However, piranhas can be a problem when introduced to new ecosystems. If piranhas weren't around, how might the Amazon be different? How might piranhas affect a river or lake in your hometown?

Tell the Tale

Imagine that you are a scientist studying piranhas in the Amazon. Write 200 words telling the story of your research expedition. What are you hoping to discover? Where do you go to find piranhas? What do the piranhas you see look like? Make sure to set the scene, develop a sequence of events, and offer a conclusion.

Say What?

Studying piranhas can mean learning a lot of new vocabulary. Find five words in this book that you've never heard before. Use a dictionary to find out what they mean. Then write the meanings in your own words and use each word in a new sentence.

Surprise Me

Learning about piranhas can be interesting and surprising. After reading this book, what two or three facts about these fish do you find most surprising? Write a few sentences about each fact. Why did you find these facts surprising?

GLOSSARY

ecosystem
the group of plants and animals living in and interacting with their environment

frenzy
wild excitement

fry
young fish

lepidophagy
a fish eating the scales of another fish

native
to live naturally in a specific place

scavenger
clean up, forage

shoal
a group of piranhas

spawn
to produce and lay eggs

species
a group of similar animals that are closely enough related to mate with one another

tributary
a stream or river that flows into a larger river

LEARN MORE

Books

Berger, Melvin and Gilda. *True or False: Dangerous Animals.* New York: Scholastic, 2009.

Colidron, Deborah. *Piranhas.* Edina, MN: ABDO, 2010.

Meister, Cari. *Amazon River.* Edina, MN: ABDO 2002.

Web Links

To learn more about piranhas, visit ABDO Publishing Company online at **www.abdopublishing.com**. Web sites about piranhas are featured on our Book Links page. These links are routinely monitored and updated to provide the most current information available.

Visit **www.mycorelibrary.com** for free additional tools for teachers and students.

INDEX

ABOUT THE AUTHOR

Ann Ingalls is the author of 20 published and forthcoming books for children, as well as dozens of poems, short stories, and nonfiction articles for magazines and the Core Knowledge Foundation.